FUN WITH SCIENCE AND TECHNOLOGY

Written by Jacky Theobald

Edited by Ann Morgan

Illustrated by Ron Branagan

Copyright © 1995
The Scout Association
Baden-Powell House, Queen's Gate, London SW7 5JS

First Edition
Printed in Great Britain by
Wednesday Press Ltd, Southend-on-Sea, Essex
Designed by Spotlight Design Services Ltd

Contents

	Page
THE BEAVER SCOUT PROGRAMME:	3
INTRODUCTION:	5
MOVEMENT:	6
ELECTRICITY:	15
CHEMICALS:	23
AIR:	32
LIGHT AND COLOUR:	44

The Beaver Scout Programme

The Beaver Scout Programme supports and promotes the planning of balanced programmes in the Colony.

It is made up of some areas of activity and a variety of methods which take place within a framework of key principles.

The Beaver Scout Programme is illustrated on the diagram overleaf and is shown as three rings, each of which is equally important.

The **Principles**, shown on the outer ring, underpin all that is done in Beaver Scouting. They describe what Beaver Scouting is all about and ensure that Colonies provide real Scouting for youngsters of Beaver Scout age.

The **Methods**, shown in the middle ring, describe how Beaver Scouts take part in the programme week by week.

The **Activity Areas**, shown in the centre of the diagram, describe what Beaver Scouts do in the programme week by week.

- Beaver Scouts learn about themselves – exploring their feelings and developing good habits of health and personal safety.
- Beaver Scouts get to know people – finding out about people in their family, the family of Scouting, the local community and the wider world.
- Beaver Scouts explore – discovering the exciting world of science, nature and technology, exploring the natural and man-made world.
- Beaver Scouts care – growing in their love of God and responding to the needs of others, the local community and the wider world.

To achieve a balanced programme, Colony Leaders are encouraged to plan at least one activity that fits into each Activity Area, at least once every three or four months. In addition, each of the methods should be used at least once during the same period.

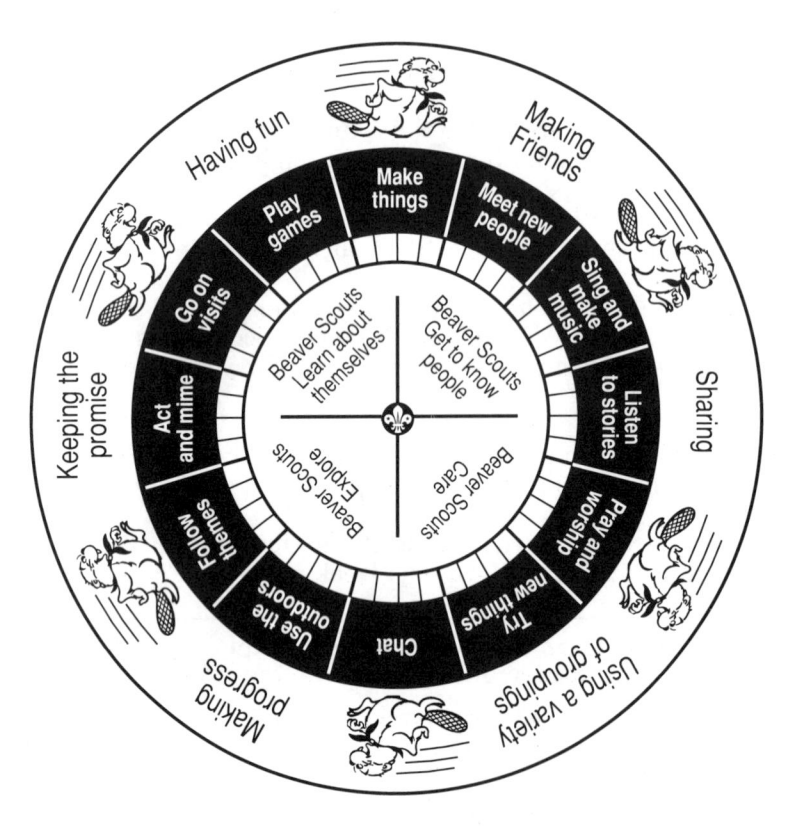

Each Activity Area can be experienced using any of the Methods. Similarly, any of the Methods can be used to introduce any Activity. Thus, the Beaver Scout Programme encourages Leaders to think of different ways to do things as well as different things to do.

Leaders are also encouraged to approach each Activity Area in a variety of ways, by including activities sometimes close to the Beaver Scouts' own experience, sometimes based in the local community and sometimes introducing them to issues in the wider world.

This booklet provides a host of activities in one or more of the Activity Areas and suggests a wide range of ways to do them drawn from the Methods in the Beaver Scout Programme.

Introduction

Science and technology open up the world to the Beaver Scout in a challenging and exciting way. Beaver Scouts can discover why the world is like it is, why the world works and what is happening to the world around them. Science and technology should be an adventure of self-discovery, achieved by active and progressive involvement. They should also be FUN.

This booklet is designed for you and your Colony to use and develop as you choose. It is up to you to pick a whole subject or mix and match ideas from this booklet or any other resource. Throughout the booklet there are a number of 'discovery points' followed by activity ideas. These will allow the Beaver Scouts to explore the scientific principles. Encourage the Beaver Scouts to ask 'why' things happen and, for your part, urge them to express their own knowledge and new discoveries.

Choose your own way of working with your Beaver Scouts; individually, in pairs, in groups or as a whole Colony.

Do not be afraid to use scientific terminology; Beaver Scouts (and adults) love learning new words.

Many of the activities lend themselves to talking about the need for personal safety and welfare and about the effects of technology on the community.

It is hoped that the ideas in this booklet are easily adaptable and accessible to any Colony, in any environment. So discover in safety and, above all, have fun together.

Movement

Objects cannot move by themselves. They need a force to push or pull, to start or stop them moving. A force called gravity, discovered by scientist Isaac Newton in the 17th Century, pulls things down to the ground. However, machines have been invented to move things in different directions and at different speeds using various methods. Rollers, wheels, levers, gears and pulleys all help to move objects by pushing, pulling, lifting, stretching, twisting and spinning.

Beaver Scouts discover

Dropped objects should land together as gravity pulls them to earth at the same speed, despite their difference in weight.

- You will need tin trays, chairs and pairs of objects, such as a sponge ball/tennis ball; a sugar cube/dice; a stone/marble; a ball bearing/ball. The Beaver Scouts stand on chairs and, holding paired objects in each hand, drop the articles at the same time onto the tray. Which one lands first?

Beaver Scouts discover

Objects have weight because gravity pulls on them. The greater the pull of gravity on a object the more it weighs. People do not feel their weight if they are floating. Bouncing on a trampoline will make you feel weightless when you are up in the air, but you are soon pulled down to earth again. Astronauts experience this feeling when they are in space because the earth's gravity gets less the further they travel from earth.

- Arrange a trampolining event at your local sports or leisure centre so that Beaver Scouts may discover this feeling.

- Make a spring balance to compare the weights of small objects, such as marbles, pencils, stones, paper, fruit, and so on. You will need yoghurt pots, string, paper clips, drawing pins, paper, rulers, pencils, and elastic bands. Compare the different weights. Perhaps older and younger Beaver Scouts could work together.

Beaver Scouts discover

Objects have a point where they are held in balance by the force of gravity. This balancing point is called the centre of gravity, for at this point the whole weight of the object is centred.

- You will need some empty shoe boxes, some weighted objects, such as modelling clay, potatoes, stones and some adhesive tape. Balance the box on the end of the table and gradually ease it over the edge. What happens? The point where it balances is the centre of gravity. Now tape a weighted object into the corner of the box and try again. What happens now? Has the centre of gravity changed?

- Let each Beaver Scout make a balancing clown or gymnast. Prepare the outlines from the illustrations below. They balance because the weight of the coins keeps the centre of gravity under the nose.

Beaver Scouts discover

When two rough or uneven surfaces rub together, an invisible force called friction holds them back and makes moving difficult. Moving is easy when there is little or no friction between surfaces.

- You will need water, soap, handcream, vegetable oil or similar, bowls and towels, screw top jars with lids, sandpaper. Let the Beaver Scouts try to open the jars with dry hands; with soapy, wet hands, after using handcream on their hands, after using vegetable oil on their hands.

What happens? Friction has been reduced making their hands move or slip over the jars and therefore making the jars less easy to open. Now try opening the jars using strips of sandpaper wrapped around the lid. What happens? Friction has been increased so the jars open.

Beaver Scouts discover

Water and oil can help to reduce friction, so can smooth surfaces. Talk about polished surfaces which help to make things slide - bowling alleys and ice rinks, for example. Oil and grease help to reduce friction and do not dry so quickly. They are used in machines such as bicycles and cars to reduce friction and form a layer between the moving parts to stop them rubbing together. Friction can create heat.

- Ask the Beaver Scouts to take note of how their hands feel. Now ask them to rub them together, slowly at first and then faster and faster. What happens? What changes do they feel?

Beaver Scouts discover

A heavy load moves more easily on rollers than sliding along the ground.

- The ancient Egyptians used slopes and rollers to construct their pyramids using tree trunks to haul up huge stones to build these monuments. You will need shoe boxes, round pencils, small lightweight objects. Place the objects in the box and push it across a floor or table top. What happens? How easily does it move? How does it feel? Now put a number of round pencils on to the surface, balance the 'filled' box on top of the pencils and try pushing the box along. The back pencils will have to be put in front of the box as it moves along. Does the box move more easily before or after using the pencil rollers?

Beaver Scouts discover

Wheels make things easier to move and are more useful than rollers. Wheels were invented about 6,000 years ago. They can be made of different materials, such as wood, plastic, rubber and metal.

- Visit a transport museum and spot how many different sorts of wheels the Beaver Scouts can find. Go for a walk and spot as many different wheels as you can. Hold a quiz, find some pictures, talk about the things which use wheels. Do some wheels move more easily than others? Discuss the reasons why this may be.

- You will need children's plastic blocks and shapes with wheel pieces. Make something which moves, using the wheels. Try making one with different sized wheels. How does it move? Now try using wheels of the same size.

Beaver Scouts discover

Pulleys are special types of wheel. A pulley has a groove around its rim for a rope to fit into it. When a heavy load is attached to one end it can be lifted more easily. Are there any cranes which use pulleys and levers at work in your locality which could be viewed, safely, in operation?

- Make a simple pulley using wire, cotton reels, string, hooks, a toy bucket full of heavy objects. Older Beaver Scouts could work with younger Beaver Scouts. Is it easy to lift the load with a pulley?

- Ask your Scout Troop or Venture Scout Unit to do some pioneering using pulleys and to invite your Beaver Scouts to try it out.

Beaver Scouts discover

A lever is one of the simplest ways of lifting or moving an object. A lever increases the pushing force under the object so it can be moved with a small effort. Levers lift objects when the resting point or pivot is close to the object and the pushing point is as far away as possible.

- You will need balls and bats. Play rounders or cricket, in a relay form of a game, using only the hands of the Beaver Scouts to hit the ball. Play until everyone has had a go and hit the ball! Now play the game using a bat. What happens to the ball? The ball will have been hit much further when the bat was used. This is because the Beaver Scouts' arms work as a lever, with their elbows acting as a pivot and their muscles providing the pushing force.

- **Make a coin jump.**

    You will need a ruler, a pencil and two coins for each Beaver Scout. Find out where to push on the ruler or lever, to get the best lift.

Beaver Scouts discover

There are many different sorts of movements; swinging, spinning, twisting, stretching. Here are some ideas to help to show these movements.

- **Make a Jumping Monster:**
  You will need 2 shapes as illustrated, a long elastic band for each Beaver Scout, scissors, felt tip pens.

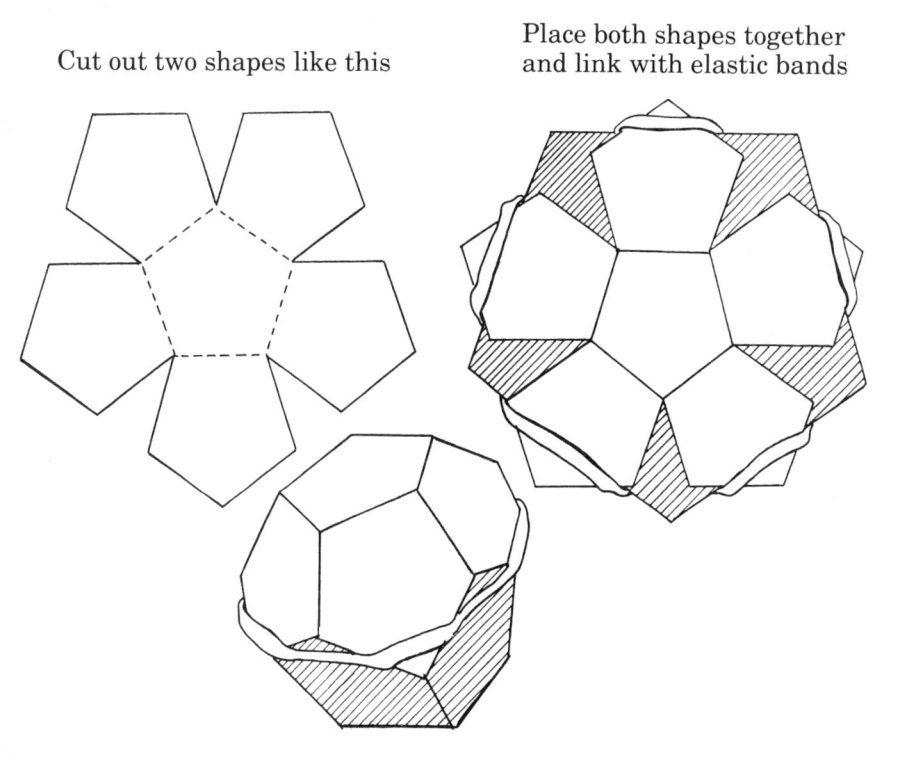

Cut out two shapes like this

Place both shapes together and link with elastic bands

Both sides will spring together.
Decorate sides with monster faces.

- The swinging movement is used in clocks in the form of a pendulum. Pendulums swing to and fro at a fixed rate so they make the clock's mechanism move at a steady speed. Does your Colony meet near a public clock with a pendulum? Go for a visit and ask a local expert to explain how it works and any other interesting facts.

- Some substances stretch when pulled, but then spring back into their original shape and size. This movement is stretching and twisting. Organise a visit to a sports or leisure centre and have a go at trampolining. The Beaver Scout body weight stretches the elastic sheet of the trampoline which springs back and flings the Beaver Scout body into the air. Remember to talk about gravity too, mentioned earlier.

- When an object spins around it creates a centrifugal force which pulls it outwards. This force is used in fairground rides and in the home in automatic washing machines and spin driers. You will need jars and marbles. Place a jar over a marble on a table. Move the jar in a quick circular motion and gradually lift it a short distance from the table's surface. The marble will spin until it is pressed against the side of the jar by centrifugal force. It will not fly out.

Electricity

Without electricity life as we know it would be very different. There would be no easy way to make light or heat, to cook or to keep clean. Electricity was first discovered by Thales, an ancient Greek, in 600BC. In 1570AD, William Gilbert, an Englishman, carried out similar experiments and called the effect electricity after Elektron, the Greek for amber. Thales' and Gilbert's experiments discovered static electricity, which does not move. However, other scientists have discovered how to make electricity move and now electricity comes to our homes every day to make our lives easier.

Beaver Scouts will have come across one form of static electricity already, probably without realising. This is 'electricity in the sky', known as lightning. During a storm giant sparks of static electricity flash across the sky; light travels quickly, 300,000 kilometres per second so that the flash is seen instantly. The sound, in this case thunder, travels more slowly, 330 metres per second. In a storm the flash of lightning is seen first and then if you count slowly, you can discover how far away the storm is. Start counting when you see the flash and every three you count, means the storm is one kilometre away.

Beaver Scouts discover

Static electricity can be made easily. Static means stationary; static electricity does not move. Plastic and nylon hold electricity better than other substances. Static electricity can be positive or negative, so an object with one kind of charge will attract an object with the opposite charge.

- **Make static electricity.**
  You will need plastic combs or blown up balloons, woollen material and scraps of tissue paper. Rub the comb/balloon several times on the fabric and hold it closely to the tissue paper. What happens?

- Rub a plastic comb/balloon on some woollen material. Hold it closely to a thin stream of water running from a tap. What happens to the water?

- Can the Colony stick balloons to a wall without using glue? Rub a balloon several times onto woollen fabric and hold it against a wall. What happens? Why? How long will the balloon stay on the wall? Now challenge the rest of your Lodge or the whole Colony to see who has the 'stickiest' balloon.

- Can you change your hair style without using a brush or comb? Rub a balloon onto woollen fabric several times and then put it near your hair. What happens?

- **Separate salt and pepper.**

   You will need, salt, pepper, plates, plastic combs or pens and woollen fabric. Sprinkle and mix together some salt and pepper on a plate. Rub the comb or pen very hard against the fabric. Hold it closely to the plate, moving it slowly. What happens? The pepper jumps up onto the pen/comb but the salt stays on the plate. Why? The salt and the pepper are attracted to the pen/comb but the pepper is lighter and finer so it is lifted more easily.

Beaver Scouts discover

Electricity in the home, at school or in the Colony meeting place is different from static electricity and it moves from place to place. It flows through wires and is called a current. An electrical current is measured in volts and is named after Volta, a 19th Century Italian scientist who discovered that metals and liquids work together to produce electricity. Beaver Scouts can discover about electrical currents safely by using small batteries and bulbs.

- **Make a battery from a lemon.**

    You will need a lemon, brass drawing pin, steel paper clip, torch bulb and electric wire. Follow the illustration to see whether the lemon can light up the bulb.

    What happens? The current flows because a chemical reaction takes place between the metals and the liquids. A commercial battery uses a chemical paste which is safely held in a metal case.

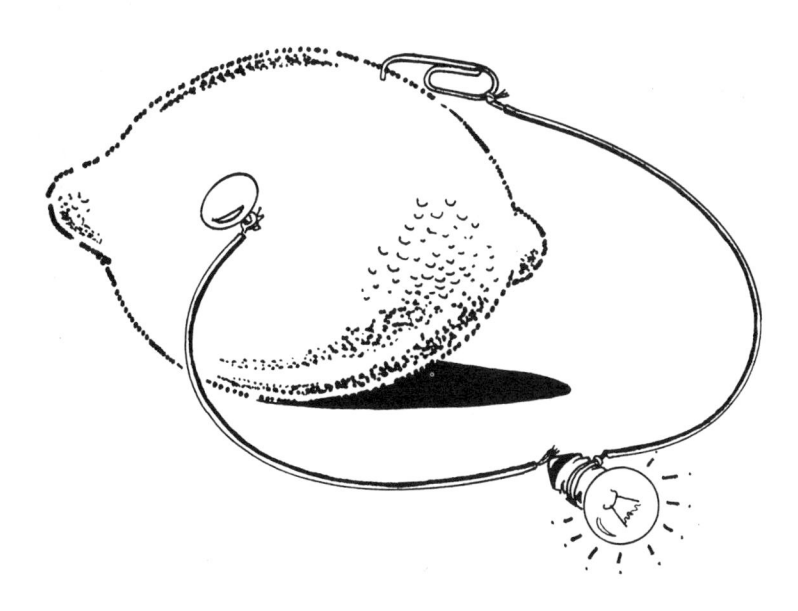

Beaver Scouts discover

Electricity needs a path to move along; a wire for example. Electricity can only move in one direction. This loop is called a circuit. If a circuit is complete, then electricity will flow, but if there is a gap, electricity will not flow.

- You will need batteries, prepared plastic wiring, small torch bulbs (less than 3 volts) and as an option, torch bulb holders and screwdrivers.

  Can you make a bulb light up? What happens? The electricity flows from one end of the battery through the bulb and back to the other end of the battery.

  What happens if Beaver Scouts link two batteries into their circuit?

  What happens if Beaver Scouts link two negative or two positive battery ends together into their circuit?

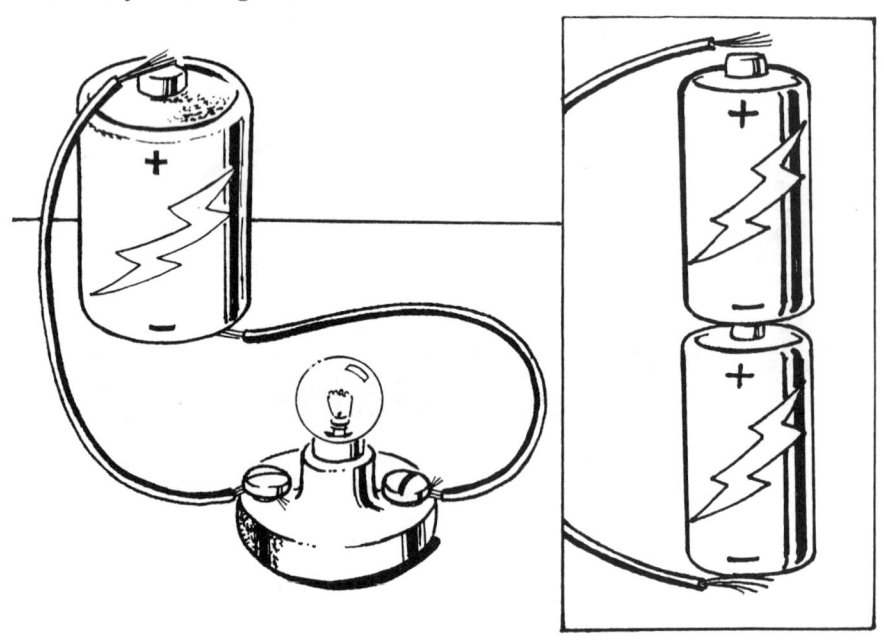

Can the Beaver Scouts link three bulbs to one battery so all three light up at the same time? Illustrated are two ways to see this work.

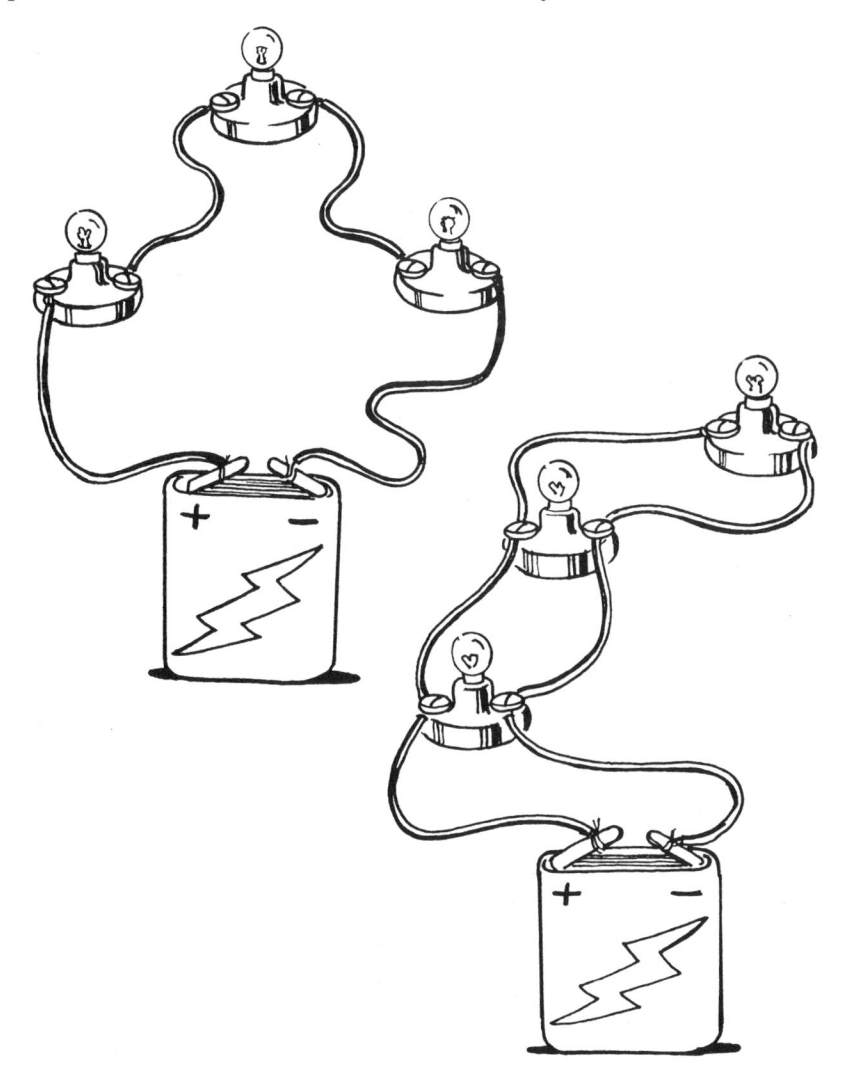

What happens when one of the light bulbs in the circuit is taken out?

19

Beaver Scouts discover

There are materials which stop electricity flowing through them. They are called insulators. Conductors carry electricity to where it is wanted and needed, for example, electrical wiring in our homes, whilst insulators stop electricity leaking where it is not needed and could be harmful, for example, switches and fuses.

- Collect a variety of objects together, such as coins, paper clips, pen tops, wooden spoons, erasers, stones, keys, paper, and so on. You will also need some electrical circuits which the Beaver Scouts could make and test before they proceed with this activity.

Touch the end of both the wires to the objects which have been collected. Does the bulb light up? Place the objects which make the bulb light up in one pile; this is the conductor pile. What are they made from? Place the objects which did not light up the bulb in another; this is the insulator pile. What are they made from?

Beaver Scouts discover

Electricity can flow through some materials. These are called conductors. A switch is a gap in the electrical circuit that can be crossed easily. When a switch is pressed on, an electrical current can flow and lights and machines will work because the gap in the circuit has been closed.

- Follow the illustration to make a switch. You will need batteries, bulbs, bulb holders, electrical wire, metal drawing pins, blocks of wood.

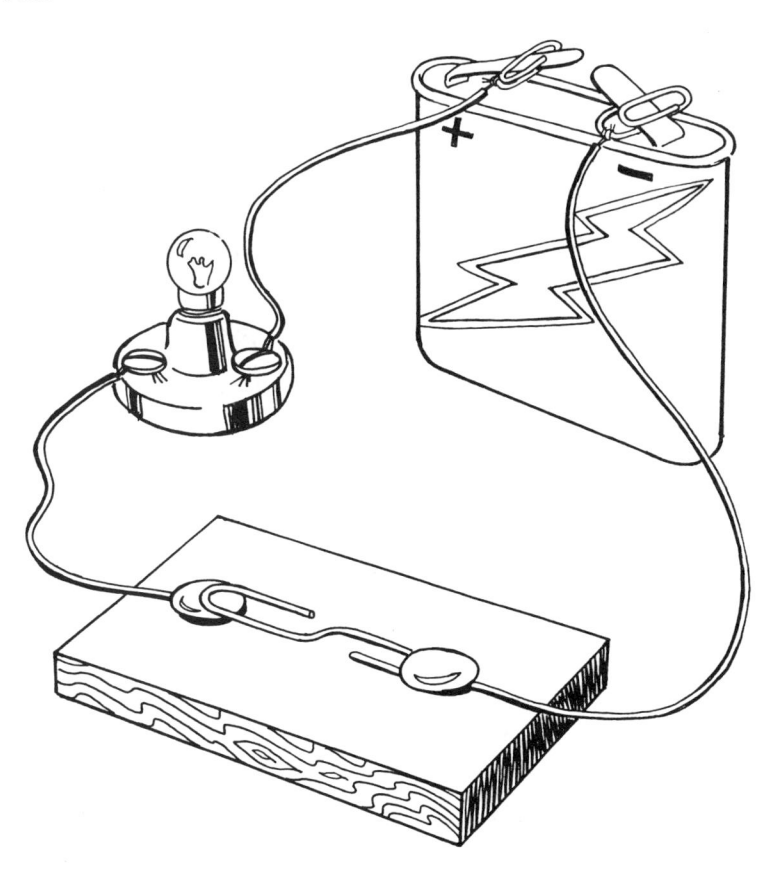

- Make a torch using an empty washing up liquid bottle. Ask some Scouts or Venture Scouts to visit the Colony to demonstrate and help the Beaver Scouts to make their own torches. The following design can be used as a model.

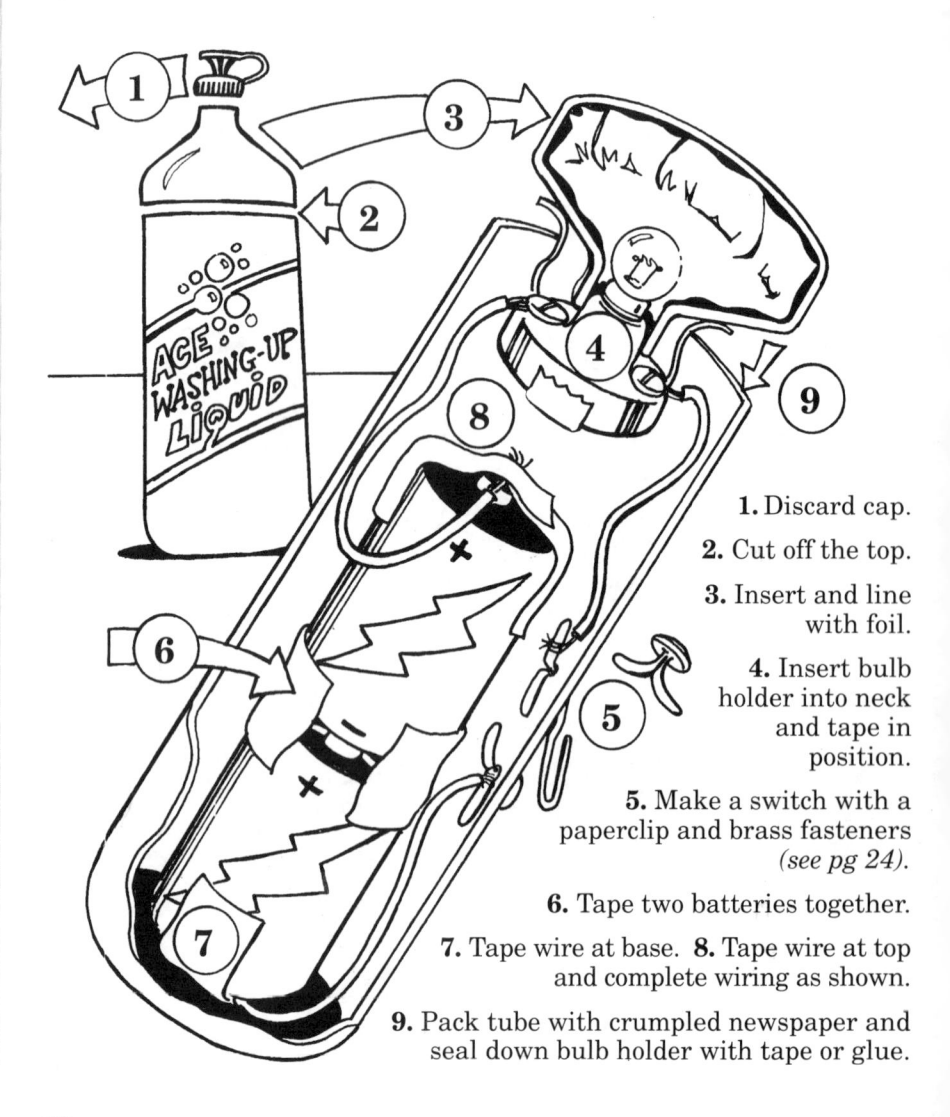

1. Discard cap.

2. Cut off the top.

3. Insert and line with foil.

4. Insert bulb holder into neck and tape in position.

5. Make a switch with a paperclip and brass fasteners *(see pg 24)*.

6. Tape two batteries together.

7. Tape wire at base. **8.** Tape wire at top and complete wiring as shown.

9. Pack tube with crumpled newspaper and seal down bulb holder with tape or glue.

Chemicals

Everything is made of chemicals - rocks, soil, homes, roads, schools, cars, plants, animals, even Beaver Scouts. There is a set of basic chemical substances from which everything is made, although things contain different proportions of these which is why they look and feel different to each other.

Chemistry is the scientific study of how these substances are joined together to form the objects and materials in the world around us. Sometimes these substances are split and sometimes they are combined to make up new chemical substances.

The chemical industry is big business and can help people enjoy a good life by making things better for everyone, for example medicines, oil, plastics, foods. However the world has only so many chemicals and care needs to be taken to preserve and maintain these resources and to protect the world from dangerous chemicals and substances.

Beaver Scouts discover

Chemicals are all around, forming everything that is smelled, touched, tasted, seen and even things which cannot be seen, for example air or glass. Chemistry is happening all the time and chemicals are changing all the time. Chemicals can be identified by using the senses, providing it is safe to do so, by looking, smelling, touching and tasting. These are simple ways to detect the chemical properties of a substance.

- Test the properties of chemicals. You will need a variety of substances. Here are some ideas:

  For tasting: salt; sugar.

  Grind up in small amounts and try to guess which is which, first by looking and then by tasting. Sugar can be bought in cubes, granulated, castor or as icing sugar. The taste is the same but the texture is different.

  For feeling: lemon juice/vegetable oil; water/melted lard; orange squash/melted margarine or butter.

Can the Beaver Scouts tell the difference by looking? Try feeling them. The oils will feel thick and slippery and the liquids will feel thin and watery.

For smelling: chopped apple/raw potato; cider vinegar/apple juice; malt vinegar/black coffee; red wine vinegar/blackcurrant squash.

Try feeling or looking. Can the Beaver Scouts identify the substances? Now try sniffing the substances to tell them apart. Smells consist of tiny particles of odour floating in the air which can be detected by the nerves in the nose. Substances may look and feel the same but may only be distinguished by their smell.

For seeing: felt tip pens/paper.

Mix up the felt tip pens and challenge the Beaver Scouts to draw a simple picture whilst blindfolded; a tree, a flower for example. How did the pictures turn out? Eyesight is an important sense because it helps people to see colour and shapes. Colour is an important property of many chemicals. It is used by nature to show danger, for example, yellow and black - wasps and bees or plants where red and black berries can be harmful for animals and humans to eat.

For weighing: collect together a variety of balls, all of the same size and preferably the same colour but made of differing substances or manufacturing processes, rubber, sponge and so on or use potatoes, stones and fruit of the same size and colour.

The items look the same but have different weights. Guess which is heaviest and lightest? Grade in weight using the hands and then by using kitchen scales. Chemicals can be very heavy for their size, for example, lead weights; or very light, for example, polystyrene items.

- You will need screw top jars, water, some nails or similar. Place a nail in a screw top jar with water and another nail in a dry screw top jar. Leave until the next Colony meeting. What has happened to the nail? The nail in the water has gone red and changed colour. It has changed because chemicals change all the time. The change can be seen on the nail because rust has formed whilst in water.

Beaver Scouts discover

Chemicals can mix together without change whilst others react together to produce a new kind of chemical. Chemicals may be mixed or dissolved with each other or be separated. When chemicals are separated they are the same as they were at the beginning, but sometimes they react to each other and it becomes more complicated and, sometimes, quite impossible to separate.

- Find out if chemicals will dissolve. You will need tap water and a variety of substances, some of which will dissolve and others which will not. Here are some ideas; tea bags, coffee, salt, sugar, honey, sand, vegetable oil. You will also need some containers and spoons. Add small amounts of the substances to a measure of clean water, renew water for each substance tested and stir slowly. What happens to the substance? Does it dissolve? If a substance is soluble it will disappear, although it may give its colour to the water. Chemicals such as sand and vegetable oil do not dissolve.

  Now try the activity using very cold water that has been stored in a refrigerator. What happens? Does the temperature of the water make a difference to the solubility of the substances. Do the chemicals dissolve better than before? If so, which ones?

  Try again! This time use very warm tap water. What happens now? Why? What are the differences between the solubility of the substances using warm, cold and ordinary tap water?

- You will need blotting paper or coffee filter paper, plates, inks or dyes (felt tip pens are excellent), water. Cut the paper into strips and generously colour one end with a blob of dye. Hang up the strips so that the ends just dip into the water on the plate. What happens? Leave for 5 minutes and allow to dry. What can the Beaver Scouts see now? The different pigments in the dye have travelled up the paper at different speeds, using capillary action. The ink has separated into different colours.

25

Beaver Scouts discover

Chemicals have properties which can be detected, for example, by smell and colour. There are other important chemical properties to detect, called acids and bases which when mixed together form salts. Acids, bases and salts and their reactions are used around the home and in industry. Acids are sour tasting. Bases taste bitter and feel slimy. Strong acids and bases are corrosive; they can 'eat away' other substances including flesh and must never be touched.

- Discover substances which are bases or acids. Before you start you will need to make an indicator by chopping up a red cabbage and boiling in water for 15 to 20 minutes. Strain and sieve the liquid and retain until cool. This is the indicator.

  Collect together a variety of household substances such as fizzy drinks, fruit squashes and juices, vinegar, condiment sauces, infused tea and coffee, flour and include bicarbonate of soda and lemon juice. You will also need plates, teaspoons and cups to put the indicator in for each Beaver Scout.

Start by mixing a teaspoon of indicator with some bicarbonate of soda. What happens? It should turn a pale greeny blue - bases turn this shade. Now try with lemon juice. What happens? It should turn pinkish red, indicating an acid. Using the indicator, try other substances and find out if they are acids or bases. How did the Beaver Scouts know which were which?

- **Make some fizzy lemonade.**

    You will need food colourings, jugs, icing sugar, bicarbonate of soda, lemon juice, water and glasses. The basic recipe for one average jug of water is to add a few drops of colouring, 2 tablespoons of icing sugar, 3 teaspoons of bicarbonate of soda and 6 tablespoons of lemon juice. Stir and mix together well. What happens? The acid (lemon juice) and the base (bicarbonate of soda) react together and make carbon dioxide (fizzy bubbles). Drink the lemonade!

    Tip: This lemonade needs to be made and drunk immediately as the fizz quickly disappears.

- You will need some discarded teeth (ask a friendly butcher) or some coins. Put the items, in jars, into condiment sauces, fizzy drinks, vinegar and so on and leave until the next Colony meeting. What has happened to the coins or the teeth? The teeth or coins will be eaten away. Too strong substances can damage and corrode. Talk about personal safety, dental and health issues.

Beaver Scouts discover

Colour is a property of many chemicals. Not all creatures can see in colour, but colours are particularly important to humans. Some chemicals have strong bright colours. Colour is made from pigments or dyes. Colour pigments are used to stain substances and help us to see the world in an exciting way.

- Try mixing colour chemicals. Use paints. You will need paint brushes, paper, paint palettes and paints in the three primary colours, red, yellow, blue plus black and white. What happens when the Beaver Scouts paint a picture mixing and using as many colours as they are able? For example, they will find that mixing red and yellow will make orange, black and white will produce grey and so on. Try using different, more or less amounts of each colour. What happens to the colour chemicals in the paint? The Beaver Scouts have created colour chemical reactions.

- You will need white paper, lemon juice, paint brushes and an iron. Paint a picture using lemon juice. Allow to dry. What has happened to the pictures? The lemon juice has become almost invisible. Use some gentle heat from a dry iron and iron the paper. What happens? The picture reappears because the heat has 'burnt' the chemical, making it visible.

Beaver Scouts discover

Electricity is generated when certain chemicals react together.

- **Split up water.**

    You will need torch batteries (flat type preferably), HB pencils, pencil sharpeners, salt, water, card, jars, electrical wire.

    Connect up the wires to the pencils which have been placed in salt water. What happens? The electricity splits the water and makes air bubbles appear around the pencil tips. Chemical changes can generate electricity and electricity can produce chemical changes, in this case by making liquid water turn to a gas. The water is split into hydrogen and oxygen which is what water is made from. This chemical change is called electrolysis and is used in the metal industry to make tin cans for storing food which we can eat later.

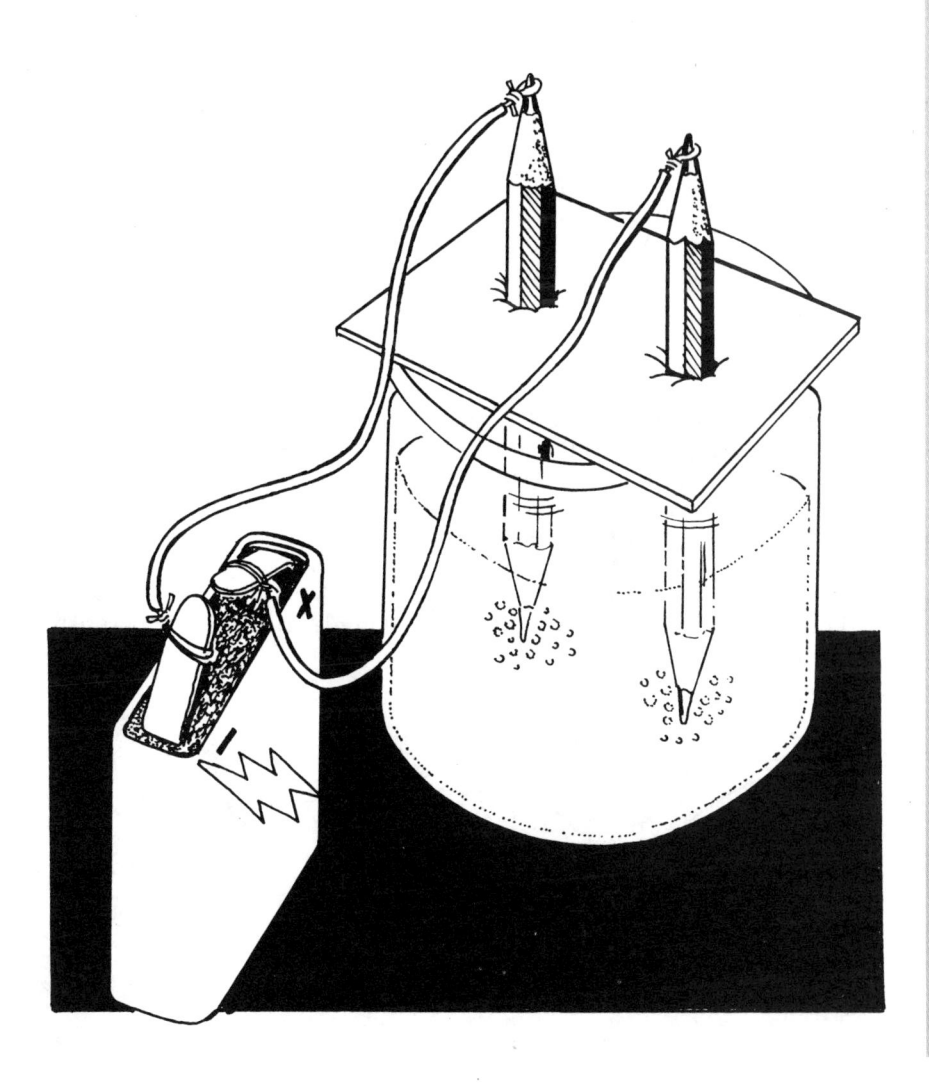

Beaver Scouts discover

Carbon chemicals are the basis of life itself. Carbons mix with other chemicals - oxygen, hydrogen, nitrogen - in different amounts to make living bodies. This is called organic chemistry. Living things need energy to power the chemical reactions in their bodies. This energy comes from the sun. The energy from the sun is stored in plants and animals and in the earth itself as oil, coal and gas.

- What does carbon look like? You will need bread or similar and/or marshmallows and a source of supervised heat.

  Try toasting or grilling and then eating the ingredients. What happens? Why? When organic chemicals are 'burnt', carbon appears as a dark substance on the outside of the food in the form of a black powder.

- **Plastic milk.**

  You will need creamy milk, saucepans and vinegar. Warm the milk to simmering point and add a few drops of vinegar. Keep stirring all the time. It will become stringy and rubbery. Allow to cool and when safe, wash under cold running water. Use sieves to prevent loss and accidents. What has happened? The milk is a carbon containing substance which has formed a 'plastic' that can be bounced or moulded into shapes. Many plastics are formed by petroleum oil. This is a carbon containing substance made from tiny sea creatures millions of years ago.

Beaver Scouts discover

Chemical reactions take place in living bodies. This is called biochemistry. These reactions can make useful substances, such as medicines and are also used in food cookery, for example, enzymes and fermentation/yeasts. The body needs the right proportions of three main types of food substances to stay healthy: Starchy, sugar foods such as breads, fruit and vegetables; fats and proteins which are found in animal products; and pulses such as beans, peas and so on. These chemicals are body building materials for repair and growth.

- **Demonstrate how enzymes work.**

    You will need two screw top jars, water, shelled hard boiled eggs, ordinary washing powder and some biological washing powder.

    Dissolve the washing powder in two jars using water. Place an egg in each jar and leave until the next Colony meeting. Take a look at the eggs. What has happened to the eggs? The enzymes in the biological powder will have 'eaten away' the organic chemicals of the egg whilst the egg in the ordinary washing powder will be unaffected. Enzymes control the speed of a biochemical reaction in a living body.

Air

Air is all around us, but is hardly noticed at all. The oxygen in the air keeps people alive when they breathe. Air can be seen when bubbles are produced under water but it is easier to see the effects of air on the surroundings. Air influences the way things happen in the world.

Take the Colony outside if you can or use pictures and/or talk about the way air affects the surroundings. Here are some things which you may see: birds and gliders using warm air currents to float; air moving to push boats and windmills; and air which is squashed - compressed air - in tyres to support lorries, cars and bicycles; air currents which move trees and grasses.

Beaver Scouts discover

Air is all around but it cannot be tasted or touched. Air does not smell but it is possible to detect smells which are carried by air; perfume, petrol fumes, cooking smells. Air is felt when it moves, for trees and plants bend and sway so the effect of the air's movement can be seen.

- Look for air. Air is all around and fills tiny spaces and gaps. You will need buckets or bowls, water, bottles, clay flower pots or similar and some soil. Push the bottles under the water and let them fill up. What happens? Why? The water rushes in and the air in the bottle escapes, making bubbles in the water. Now try using the clay pots and then the soil. What do the Beaver Scouts see? How much air did they contain? Which contains the most and the least air?

Beaver Scouts discover

Air has a weight, although it cannot be seen or touched.

- You will need balloons, canes, adhesive tape, pencils, tins. Organise the activity as illustrated without blowing up the balloons. Does the stick remain level? This means the balloons weigh the same. Blow up one of the balloons and fix it back onto the stick. Does the stick still balance? The full balloon makes the stick dip down. This shows that it is heavier than the empty balloon and that the air inside does weigh something.

- Make a submarine using a plastic bottle, modelling clay, plastic tubing and adhesive tape. How does the submarine work? As it is filled with air, which weighs less than water, it rises to the surface.

Beaver Scouts discover

Hot air rises as it is lighter than cold air. This causes currents of air to move around.

- Making a spinning snake is a good way of observing rising air. Hang the snake above a radiator or safe source of heat. What happens? Why? It will spin as the warm air rises. For older Beaver Scouts try making a sparkling snake using tin foil.

CUT FROM PAPER OR THIN CARD.

Beaver Scouts discover

Hot air takes up more space than cold air.

- You will need plastic bottles, bowls, balloons, hot water and ice. Fit the balloons over the mouths of the bottles. Stand the bottles either in hot water or in the ice water. Wait a few minutes to see what happens.

  The air in the bottles standing in hot water has been warmed up and has expanded so it has stretched the balloons. What has happened to the balloons in the ice bowls?

- Ask the Scouts or Venture Scouts to help the Beaver Scouts make a hot air balloon using tissue paper. Inflate the balloon with hot air from a hair drier. It should float to the ceiling due to being lighter than the air around it.

Beaver Scouts discover

Warm things cool down if they are left in cold air because heat travels from warm things into cold air.

- You will need four jars with lids, hot water, newspaper, woollen scarves, elastic bands, boxes and thermometers. Remove the lids and wrap the jars up in different layers and types of materials. Fill each jar with hot water and replace the lids. Leave for 30 minutes and then take the temperature of the water in the jars. Which jar has the warmest water? The protection the jars have is called insulation which keeps air trapped in layers between the water and the cool air. This helps to prevent heat escaping.

37

Relate this experiment to layers of clothing worn by the Beaver Scouts.

Beaver Scouts discover

There is more than a kilogramme of air pressure against every 1cm of skin. The pressure is caused by a layer of air called atmosphere. When swimming under water, this effect can be felt as water pushes against the body. This is rather like the air pressure but with air everyone is used to it.

- Go for a swim with parents or as a Group activity and feel the 'push' of water against the skin.

- Air pressure is a powerful force. You will need rulers, large sheets of paper and a table. Lay the ruler on the table so one third lies over the edge. Spread the paper over the ruler. Now hit the ruler to make the paper fly in the air. It's impossible, because air presses down on the sheet of paper. The paper is large so there is a lot of air pushing against it. The ruler cannot move the paper.

- Show the Beaver Scouts how to turn a glass of water upside down without spilling any. What happens? The pressure, or the pushing power of the air keeps the water in the glass. Try this challenge over a sink or bucket first!

Beaver Scouts discover

Air can be squashed into a small space. This is called compressed air.

- You will need some plastic bags or balloons, and piles of books. The Beaver Scouts place the balloons on a table, pile books on top of them and blow up the balloons. The books will rise off the table as they are supported by compressed air.

- Make an air powered boat.

  You will need long balloons, adhesive tape, polystyrene trays and a paddling pool filled with water. What happens when the air in the balloon is released? It pushes the boat across the water.

- Make an air powered rocket.

  You will need washing up liquid bottles, plastic straws with different diameters, modelling clay, card and glue. How far can the rocket travel?

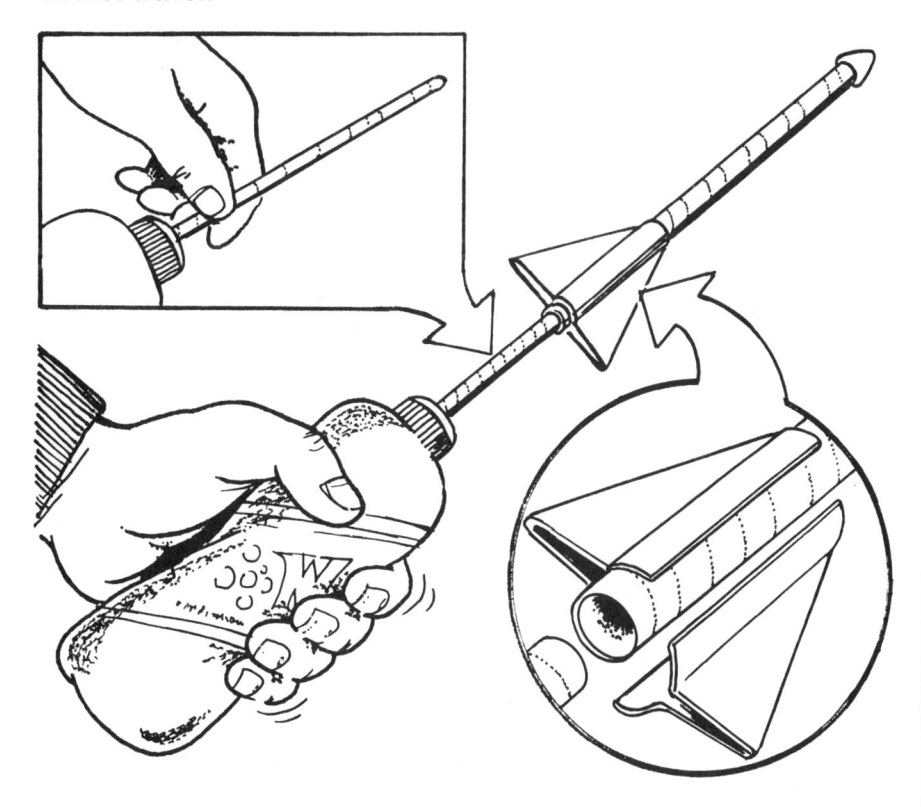

- Make some kites or borrow a variety of kites. Make and use different designs and shapes. Try flying them and see if they fly differently. What sort of wind is there, light, breezy, strong? Does this make a difference? Do some kites fly better on certain days? Ask parents or Venture Scouts to help with this activity - you may have a specialist club in your community which can demonstrate the skills of successful kite making and flying.

Beaver Scouts discover

Air is used up when things burn. However, only part of the air is burnt. This part is called oxygen and is the part of air which people need to breath and live. The rest of the air is mainly a gas called nitrogen.

- You will need candles, modelling clay, bowls of water, glass jars, and matches. Make sure the candle is tall enough to clear the water and remind the Beaver Scouts to mark the water level before they start. Light the candles. What can the Beaver Scouts see? What happens? The flame goes out when the oxygen is used and water is pushed up into the jar by the pressure of air outside.

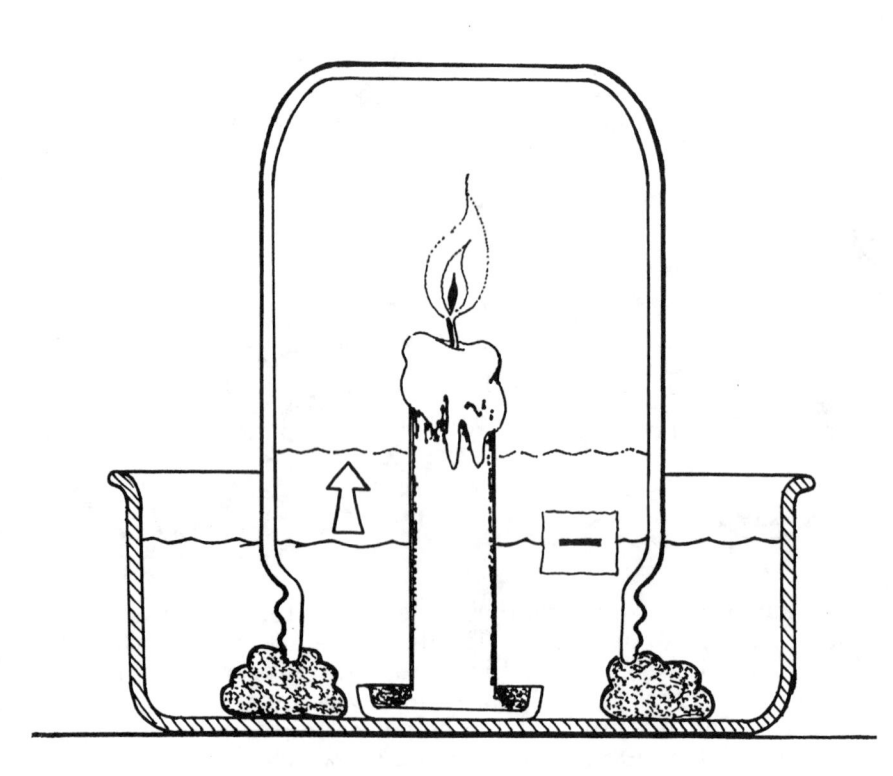

Beaver Scouts discover

All living things need oxygen to live.

- Talk about places which do not have enough oxygen, such as mountains, or no air at all, like outer space or under water. People have to take their own air supplies with them if they visit or travel to these places. Talk about personal safety and situations which can prevent air reaching the lungs, such as fires, smoke inhalation and choking.

- Find out about artificial resuscitation. Borrow or use a 'Resusci Annie' from your local first aid and rescue organisation. Ask if their trained officers would visit the Colony to explain and demonstrate this technique.

Light and Colour

Life on Earth would come to an end without sunlight from the Sun. Green plants need sunlight to make food and all animals on Earth depend on plants for food. Light can be made naturally by the Sun and by artificial means such as electricity and fire. Where no light falls, shadows are formed.

Light is made up of several different colours which can be seen in a rainbow. The colour of things around depends on which colours are reflected back into the eye.

Sunlight can be used as a form of energy, to give heat and light in homes and schools using solar panels generally found on roofs and sides of buildings. Laser machines can strengthen light energy to produce laser beams which are so powerful they can cut holes in steel. Laser beams are used by doctors operating in hospitals and can carry signals to machines such as video disc players.

Beaver Scouts discover

Light can pass through some substances. When light can be seen through something like water, it is called transparent. Other substances, such as paper and metal for instance, stop light passing through them and are called opaque. Light cannot bend around corners and only travels in straight lines. Therefore, when light shines on something which is opaque, shadows appear behind the substance.

- Using torches, darken a room and test a variety of objects. What shapes do they make? Try using the Beaver Scouts' hands. Can they make animal shapes? What happens when the objects or hands are near the light? Further away? A shape nearer the light blocks out more light so that the shadow is longer and vice versa.

Beaver Scouts discover

Light can hit a surface or an object and bounce off again. This is called reflection.

- You will need some large mirrors. Ask the Beaver Scouts to wave at themselves. Which hand is the Beaver Scout's reflection using? Mirrors reverse images. In pairs, ask the Beaver Scouts to be each others' reflections and follow their partner's movements for a short while.

- Ideally you will need some large mirrors for this activity. (Alternatively, use small mirrors and suitably sized toys or objects.) Stand the Beaver Scouts in front of the mirrors which are angled side by side. How many reflections can they see? Light is reflected from one mirror to the other. Now try moving the mirrors closer together and/or further apart. What happens? Place the mirrors so that they face each other with the Beaver Scout in the space between. What can the Beaver Scout see? Endless reflections as the light bounces to and fro between the mirrors.

- Make a kaleidoscope. Use mirrors or mirror paper, adhesive tape and some small beads. The illustration will guide you through the process. The patterns are achieved by light bouncing between the mirrors inside.

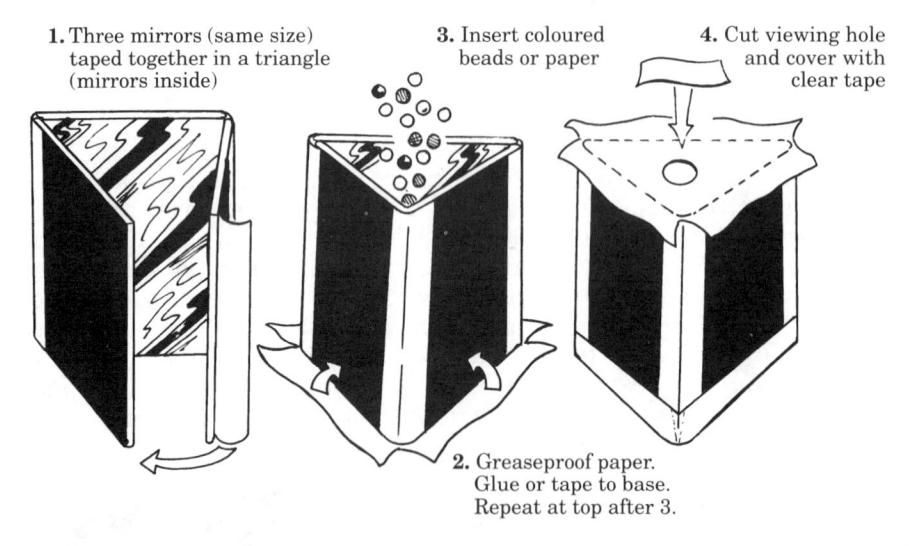

1. Three mirrors (same size) taped together in a triangle (mirrors inside)

2. Greaseproof paper. Glue or tape to base. Repeat at top after 3.

3. Insert coloured beads or paper

4. Cut viewing hole and cover with clear tape

Beaver Scouts discover

Light travels at different speeds through different substances. It slows down and changes direction slightly as it goes through the substance. This is called refraction. It makes light rays look as if they bend.

- You will need glasses of water and pencils. Place the pencils into the glasses of water. What can be seen? Ask the Beaver Scouts to describe the pencils. Do they look bent? Now take the pencils out of the water. Are they bent? The light rays changed direction when they entered the water and made them look bent.

- You will need some thick glass and some pencils.

  Hold the pencil so half is above the glass and half is below. What happens to the lower part? The pencil will be seen to be separated from the part of the pencil in the air. The glass makes the light rays change direction and appears to bend the pencil.

Beaver Scouts discover

Light rays can be refracted by using transparent materials. Lenses can make objects look larger or smaller depending on their shape; concave or convex.

- Using water, make a lens to make things look larger. You will need card, clear adhesive tape and scissors. Look at a leaf or a page of a newspaper. What can the Beaver Scout see? What has happened to the object? The object looks bigger.

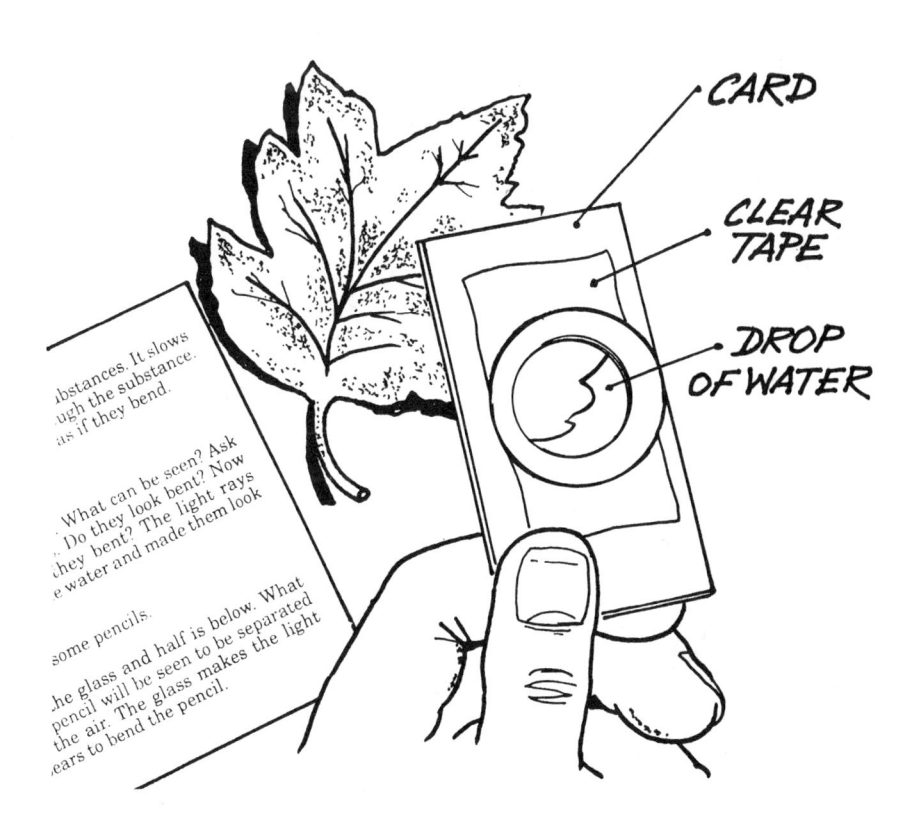

Beaver Scouts discover

Humans have two eyes which are in different positions. This allows people to see things in three-dimensions as well as to judge distance and perspective. The eyes send messages to the brain and can stop too much light damaging the delicate tissue and sensitive layers of the eye.

- Stay in a dimly lit or nearly darkened room for several minutes, perhaps use this time for a Colony chat. Ask the Beaver Scouts to look at each others' eyes and tell each other what they see. Turn the lights on and ask them to look again and see if the eyes of the other Beaver Scout have changed. How? In the dim light, the dark pupil of the eye has opened wide to let in as much light as possible in an attempt to improve sight. In bright light the pupil will become smaller to prevent too much light damaging sensitive eye tissue.

- Making holes in the hand!

    You will need cardboard tubing or paper rolled into tubes. The Beaver Scouts will see a hole in their hand because the brain is confused and so it combines the two images together to create this gory effect!

48

- Collect some Magic 3-D posters. These are published as posters, in books and in newspapers. Ask the Beaver Scouts what they can see. Can everyone see the magic pictures? Not everyone will be able to.

- Draw a dot on a piece of paper. Ask the Beaver Scouts to put one hand over one eye and use the other hand to try to touch the dot, using a pencil. Sit 75cm from the dot. What results do the Beaver Scouts have?

Beaver Scouts discover

Light appears to be colourless and is called 'white light'. This is not so, for it is made up of a mixture of colours. The colours can be separated into a rainbow pattern called a spectrum. A spectrum consists of red, orange, yellow, green, blue, indigo and violet. There are two kinds of light which humans cannot see, ultra violet and infra red.

- On a warm, sunny day devise some water activities and games for the Beaver Scouts. Adjust the nozzle of a hosepipe to make a fine mist of water and make sure that you stand with your back to the sun. The Beaver Scouts will see a rainbow in the mist of water droplets. Or look for a special moment when the weather conditions are just right and show the Beaver Scouts a rainbow.

- Can the Beaver Scouts make white light?

    You will need thin card, scissors, cocktail sticks or similar, felt tip pens, coloured pencils or crayons in the colours of the spectrum. What happens when the circle is spun quickly? The eyes cannot see each colour separately and the mixed result appears greyish/white.

- Make some more coloured circles. Use only two colours, for example, red and blue, yellow and red, blue and yellow. What are the colours of the circles when they are spun or whirled? Try other colour combinations and see what other colours can be made.

Beaver Scouts discover

The colour of an object depends on the colour of the light which is reflected back into the eyes. This could be opaque - no light reflects through; transparent - light passes through; or translucent - when some light passes through but it is blurred. Transparent materials can be coloured. This changes the colour of the objects which are seen through them.

- Make a pair of glasses and see red, yellow, blue or purple.

  You will need card, coloured cellophane, glue or adhesive tape and scissors. Put the glasses on and look around. What do the Beaver Scouts notice? How have things changed? Try different colours of cellophane spectacles. Which colours make them feel happy or sad, warm or cold?

- You will need some torches and a collection of objects or articles that are opaque, transparent and translucent, for example, paper, pottery, china, metal, glass and clear plastic of various thicknesses, tracing paper, various fabrics, tissue paper and so on. Can the Beaver Scouts sort out the collection into piles which are opaque, transparent and translucent without using a torch and then check their guesses, using a torch? Were their guesses right?

- Try some tie-dyeing. Use cotton materials in preference as they absorb dye very successfully but try other fabrics too to discover the differences. Dye T-shirts or pillowcases. What happens? The tight threads and elastic keep the dye away from the material and stay white or the original colour and make flower shaped patterns.

Beaver Scouts discover
Green plants need light to make their food, without it they would die.

- You will need strong cardboard or similar, stones, a jar, a patch of grass. Lay a piece of card onto the grass and weigh down with stones. Place the jar, upside down, near the cardboard. Leave until the next Colony meeting and then remove cardboard and jar. What has happened? What does the grass look like under the cardboard and under the jar? The grass under the cardboard looks yellow and unhealthy and the grass under the jar has grown taller than elsewhere. Where else have the Beaver Scouts seen this happen? Perhaps after a Family Camp, where tents have been pitched or under fallen branches or under stones. This activity is best carried out during the warmer months of the year, the growing season.

Beaver Scouts discover
Sunlight contains two rays, called ultra violet and infra red rays. These invisible rays can burn the skin if they are too strong. Sunlight warms the earth naturally, without it life itself would not exist. It takes longer to warm water than land.

- You will need two containers, one with sand or soil and one with water, two thermometers and a sunny, warm day.

  Place the thermometers in the containers and measure the temperature. Older Beaver Scouts would enjoy this responsibility. Now hold a Colony meeting and towards the end of the meeting check the temperatures again. What has happened to the water and to the sand? Is there a difference in temperature?

  Next time the Colony visit the seaside ask the Beaver Scouts how the sand and then the sea water feels on their feet.

Booklets in this series include

Eat without heat

Everyone is special

Five minute fillers

It's a wonderful world

Let's be safe

Let's pretend

Music is fun

We promise

Exploring the environment

Looking at your community

The beaver

Exploring prayer and worship

Fun with science and technology

Notes

notes